Also by Sally Kirkman

SALLY KIRKMAN

Capricorn

The Art of Living Well and Finding
Happiness According to Your Star Sign

HODDER

First published in Great Britain in 2018 by Hodder & Stoughton
An Hachette UK company

5

Copyright © Sally Kirkman 2018

The right of Sally Kirkman to be identified as the Author of the
Work has been asserted by her in accordance with the Copyright,
Designs and Patents Act 1988.

All images © Shutterstock.com

A CIP catalogue record for this title is available from the British Library

Hardback ISBN 978 1 473 67688 6

Typeset in Celeste 11.5/17 pt by Palimpsest Book Production Limited,
Falkirk, Stirlingshire

Printed and bound in Great Britain by Clays Ltd, Elcograf S.p.A.

Hodder & Stoughton policy is to use papers that are natural,
renewable and recyclable products and made from wood grown in
sustainable forests. The logging and manufacturing processes are expected
to conform to the environmental regulations of the country of origin.

Hodder & Stoughton Ltd
Carmelite House
50 Victoria Embankment
London EC4Y 0DZ

www.hodder.co.uk

Contents

• • • • •

Introduction

• • • • •

Before computers, books or a shared language, people were fascinated by the movement of the stars and planets. They created stories and myths around them. We know that the Babylonians were one of the first people to record the zodiac, a few hundred years BC.

In ancient times, people experienced a close connection to the earth and the celestial realm. The adage 'As above, so below', that the movement of the planets and stars mirrored life on earth and human affairs, made perfect sense. Essentially, we were all one, and ancient people sought symbolic meaning in everything around them.

We are living in a very different world now, in

which scientific truth is paramount; yet many people are still seeking meaning. In a world where you have an abundance of choice, dominated by the social media culture that allows complete visibility into other people's lives, it can be hard to feel you belong or find purpose or think that the choices you are making are the right ones.

It's this calling for something more, the sense that there's a more profound truth beyond the objective and scientific, that leads people to astrology and similar disciplines that embrace a universal truth, an intuitive knowingness. Today astrology has a lot in common with spirituality, meditation, the Law of Attraction, a desire to know the cosmic order of things.

Astrology means 'language of the stars' and people today are rediscovering the usefulness of ancient wisdom. The universe is always talking to you; there are signs if you listen and the more you tune in, the more you feel guided by life. This is one of astrology's significant benefits, helping you to make sense of an increasingly unpredictable world.

Used well, astrology can guide you in making the best possible decisions in your life. It's an essential skill in your personal toolbox that enables you to navigate the ups and downs of life consciously and efficiently.

About this book

Astrology is an ancient art that helps you find meaning in the world. The majority of people to this day know their star sign, and horoscopes are growing increasingly popular in the media and online.

The modern reader understands that star signs are a helpful reference point in life. They not only offer valuable self-insight and guidance, but are indispensable when it comes to understanding other people, and living and working together in harmony.

This new and innovative pocket guide updates the ancient tradition of astrology to make it relevant and topical for today. It distils the wisdom of the star signs into an up-to-date format that's easy to read and digest, and fun and informative too. Covering a broad range of topics, it offers you insight and understanding into many different areas of your life. There are some unique sections you won't find anywhere else.

The style of the guide is geared towards you being able to maximise your strengths, so you can live well and use your knowledge of your star sign to your advantage. The more in tune you are with your zodiac sign, the higher your potential to lead a happy and fulfilled life.

The guide starts with a quick introduction to your star sign, in bullet point format. This not only reveals your star sign's ancient ruling principles, but brings astrology up-to-date, with your star sign mission, an appropriate quote for your sign and how best to describe your star sign in a tweet.

The first chapter is called 'Be True To Your Sign' and is one of the most important sections in the guide. It's a comprehensive look at all aspects of your star sign, helping define what makes you special, and explaining how the rich symbolism of your zodiac sign can reveal more about your character. For example, being born at a specific time of year and in a particular season is significant in itself.

This chapter focuses in depth on the individual attributes of your star sign in a way that's positive and uplifting. It offers a holistic view of your sign and is meant to inspire you. Within this section, you find out the reasons why your star sign traits and characteristics are unique to you.

There's a separate chapter towards the end of the guide that takes this star sign information to a new level. It's called 'Your Cosmic Gifts and Talents' and tells you what's individual about you from your star sign perspective. Most importantly, it highlights your skills and strengths, offering you clear examples of how to make the most of your natural birthright.

The guide touches on another important aspect of your star sign, in the chapters entitled 'Your Shadow Side' and 'Your Star Sign Secrets'. This reveals the potential weaknesses inherent within your star sign, and the tricks and habits you can fall into if you're not aware of them. The star sign secrets might surprise you.

There's guidance here about what you can focus on to minimise the shadow side of your star sign, and this is linked in particular to your opposite sign of the zodiac. You learn how opposing forces complement each other when you hold both ends of the spectrum, enabling them to work together.

Essentially, the art of astrology is about how to find balance in your life, to gain a sense of universal or cosmic order, so you feel in flow rather than pulled in different directions.

Other chapters in the guide provide revealing information about your love life and sex life. There are cosmic tips on how to work to your star sign strengths so you can attract and keep a fulfilling relationship, and lead a joyful sex life. There's also a guide to your love compatibility with all twelve star signs.

Career, money and prosperity is another essential section in the guide. These chapters offer you vital information on your purpose in life, and how to make the most of your potential out in the world. Your star sign skills and strengths are revealed, including what sort of job or profession suits you.

There are also helpful suggestions about what to avoid and what's not a good choice for you. There's a list of traditional careers associated with your star sign, to give you ideas about where you can excel in life if you require guidance on your future direction.

Also, there are chapters in the book on practical matters, like your health and well-being, your food and diet. These recommend the right kind of exercise for you, and how you can increase your vitality and nurture your mind, body and soul, depending on your star sign. There are individual yoga poses and tarot cards that have been carefully selected for you.

Further chapters reveal unique star sign information about your image and style. This includes whether there's a particular fashion that suits you, and how you can accentuate your look and make the most of your body.

There are even chapters that can help you decide where to go on holiday and who with, and how to decorate your home. There are some fun sections, including ideal gifts for your star sign, and ideas for films, books and music specific to your star sign.

Also, the guide has a comprehensive birthday section so you can find out which famous people share your birthday. You can discover who else is born under your star sign, people who may be your role models and whose careers or gifts you can aspire to. There are celebrity examples throughout the guide too, revealing more about the unique characteristics of your star sign.

At the end of the guide, there's a Question and Answer section, which explains the astrological terms used in the guide. It also offers answers to some general questions that often arise around astrology.

This theme is continued in a useful section entitled Additional Information. This describes the symmetry of astrology and shows you how different patterns connect the twelve star signs. If you're a beginner to astrology, this is your next stage, learning about the elements, the modes and the houses.

View this book as your blueprint, your guide to you and your future destiny. Enjoy discovering astrological revelations about you, and use this pocket guide to learn how to live well and find happiness according to your star sign.

A QUICK GUIDE TO CAPRICORN

• • • • •

Capricorn Birthdays: 22 December to 20 January

Zodiac Symbol: The Goat-Fish

Ruling Planet: Saturn

Mode/Element: Cardinal Earth

Colour: Dark colours; grey, brown

Part of the Body: Bones, joints and teeth

Day of the Week: Saturday

Top Traits: Ambitious, Traditional, Dignified

Your Star Sign Mission: to stay true to the core principles of respect and responsibility, to honour tradition

Best At: long-term planning, building lasting investments, gaining status or responsibility, being respectful, modelling dignity, maturing like a fine wine, appreciating solitude

Weaknesses: gloomy and pessimistic, views the glass as half empty, fearful, lacks spontaneity, rigid

Key Phrase: I succeed

Capricorn Quote: 'Your reputation is more important than your pay check, and your integrity is worth more than your career.' Ryan Freitas

How to describe Capricorn in a Tweet: Briefcase at the ready, workaholic of the zodiac. Likes wine, climbing mountains, rules & boundaries. Looks younger when older

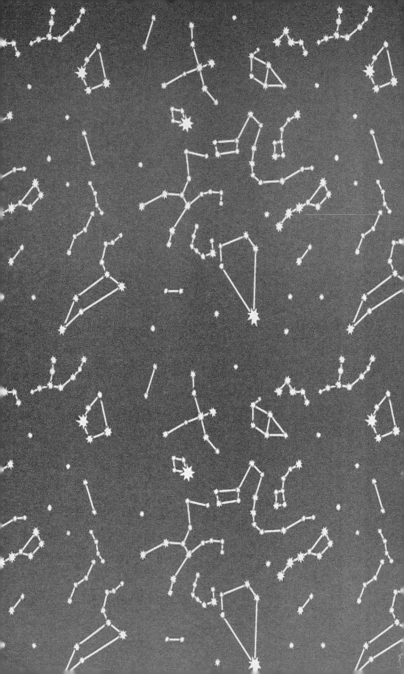

Be True To Your Sign

• • • • •

Capricorn has a reputation for being the work-aholic of the zodiac. Yes, you are typically hard-working, disciplined and ambitious, but there's more to the Capricorn nature. One of the wisest of the star signs, you approach your life with a deadpan humour and sense of irony. You understand the power of commitment, you recognise authority and you are a respectful member of society.

Born in the depths of winter in the northern hemisphere, the sign of Capricorn begins at the Winter Solstice, the shortest day and the longest night. This is the quiet time of year when it's cold and dark, and you have to be built strong and sturdy to survive. It's fitting that you are one of the hardiest signs of the zodiac, known for your ability to overcome adversity, prepared to knuckle down and do whatever it takes to survive and succeed in life.

It helps too that you are a cardinal sign, one of the markers of the seasons, and a leader and initiator of the zodiac. You need to have something to motivate you in life, to keep striving for. You honour the past, but your holy grail is the future.

Your ruling planet is Saturn, one of the most important planets in traditional astrology. Saturn represents endings and, before the modern planets were discovered, was the boundary of the universe, the planet furthest away from the Sun. In Greek mythology, Saturn is called Chronos, meaning 'Time', and another name for the planet is 'Old Father Time'.

The typical Capricorn is born an old soul. Sometimes you look older than you are or you have an old head on young shoulders. You might deal with hardship at a young age, be scared or know fear, or be taught harsh lessons about authority and discipline. You may feel lonely as a child, but all of this is potentially preparing you for success later in life.

Born into the Capricorn herd, you learn how to be patient, how to resist short-term gratification in place of long-term gain, how to build for the future and how to invest yourself fully in your long-term plans.

This is part of your earth sign heritage, as the element of earth is practical and grounded, and deals with real-life issues to do with security and progress. Earth signs, like yourself, don't rush through life. You take your time, move slowly and in so doing, learn to savour the sweeter moments.

One ending that comes to us all in life is death, and one of Saturn's roles is to remind you of your mortality. You have but one life, Saturn says, so ensure you live it well and pursue a life of accomplishment. The ultimate Capricorn goal is to live wisely and to learn from your life experience, mistakes and all.

There is a side of the Capricorn nature that taps into the darker side of Saturn, also called 'the enemy of the lights'. If you have a propensity for 'doom and gloom' thinking, you will know too well the dark side of your Capricorn nature.

You may recognise that when darkness descends, it becomes even more important to seek out the light and find your purpose in life. This is when self-mastery is called for, to keep going in the face of fear, obstacles or limitation, to harness your inner strength and focus.

The classic Capricorn is both sensible and responsible, with a leaning towards duty and commitment. You are readying yourself to take on the mantle of adulthood and authority in life when the time is right.

Capricorn rules the tenth house in astrology, which represents career prospects, status and reputation. It's the peak of the astrology wheel and signifies what you can achieve in the public eye and where you're heading, your future goals. At your best, you are one of life's high achievers.

Your sign more than any other matures like a fine wine, and the good news for Capricorn is that as you age you often still look young. In fact, many Capricorns come into their own late in life, and you are renowned for your staying power and longevity. You are the zodiac's late bloomer.

Your zodiac symbol is the Goat-Fish, part mountain goat, part sea creature. The mountain goat proceeds cautiously, yet nimbly, over the rocky terrain and defeats any obstacles in its path to reach the top of the mountain. Persistence and pluckiness win the day, both qualities that Capricorn has in abundance.

Mountains often play a significant role in your psyche too, as you are at your best when you have a metaphorical mountain to climb. When you reach the top of the mountain, you survey the terrain in front of you and think 'What now?' You might be wiser and more knowledgeable for the experience you've gained, but you're always looking for your next mountain and what lies ahead.

You rarely do anything in life because you want fame and fortune. Instead, you are impressed by knowledge and status, and you like to prove to yourself that, if you work hard, you can achieve anything. You do things by the book, you play by the rules and you take the long route to success rather than trust in luck or risk everything on the roll of a dice.

There is another side to the Capricorn archetype that is often not seen but is equally significant. The 'fish' half of your zodiac symbol reveals your hidden depths as it taps into the realm of water, representing the collective unconscious, where wisdom and spiritual knowledge reside.

Your earth symbol, the mountain goat, represents the material world and all that's tangible, whereas your water symbol, the fish's tail, signifies the subconscious and what's hidden. Deep within every Capricorn, a shamanic soul is waiting to be discovered, and you access this part of yourself through solitude and silence.

The classic Capricorn is dignified and respectful of tradition and convention. You live by a strong moral code and have a high level of integrity. You might seem cool and reserved to others, but there's more to conservative Capricorn than first meets the eye.

Your Shadow Side

One of the insults often thrown at your sign of Capricorn is that you're boring. Admittedly you are someone who moves slowly and steadily with a measured response to life's ups and downs. It takes a lot to disrupt or unsettle your stoic attitude to life.

You're also one of life's introverts, and you don't like to be drawn into crisis or drama. You're a cool character, reserved and humble rather than gushing and egotistical. You seek approval for your achievements, but the usual Capricorn response is not to congratulate yourself wildly when you reach your chosen goal.

You do, however, have to be careful that your modest and selfless behaviour doesn't dominate to such an extent that you miss out. If you don't pat yourself on the back when attaining a personal goal, you won't feel the pleasure and joy that comes from hitting your targets in life.

In psychological terms, this leaves the circle of accomplishment incomplete because the final stage is self-congratulation. If this is missing, you immediately crack on with another goal or ambitious project and drive yourself to keep achieving, always searching for that elusive feeling of self-fulfilment.

There is a deeper element to Capricorn's shadow side that kicks in when you let your inner critic take hold. Your ruling planet Saturn is known as the taskmaster of the heavens and if anyone can beat themselves up over what they've not achieved or what they've done wrong, it's Capricorn.

The mantle of guilt can be a heavy burden and if it remains in place for too long, you sink into inertia and become rigid and depressed. Any problem becomes overwhelming and fear takes hold. Saturn's legacy then exposes your own and life's limitations, holding you back, leaving you unable to move.

At its most extreme, you sink into an existence without fun, warmth or vitality. Saturn blots out the light and the side of your character that's serious and pessimistic takes hold.

This is where you can learn from your opposite sign of Cancer, a touchy-feely water sign: water rules the emotions in astrology. Cancer's feelings are often in flux, and they flow with life, both up and down. Their emotions ebb and flow, which helps them to connect with other people, to be vulnerable and intimate.

Being a Capricorn, you have to learn to let your guard down and allow other people to warm you up, to bring fun and joy into your life, to remind you of all that's possible when you live vibrantly and spontaneously. Don't become so cold and reserved and focused on work goals that you forget to nurture your inner self and let other people in.

Your Star Sign Secrets

Shhh, don't tell anyone but your greatest fear is that you won't amount to anything. You worry that if other people see beneath your air of responsibility and status in life, they'll discover you're useless. Once you stop seeking approval from outside of yourself and focus on what you are capable of rather than what you're not, the fear of being a failure fades. Strengthen your inner self and don't let the belief that you're useless disempower you. This is Capricorn's star sign secret.

You have another secret too, which is that despite your appearance of respectability, there's a part of your Capricorn nature that wants to break the rules and go wild and crazy. Some of you manage to do this in real life, but for others, it remains a fantasy that exists only in your dreams and behind closed doors. Let's call it your 'rock star' alter ego, which is ready to live large and indulge in all things sinful and illegal.

Your Love Life

Knowing about your star sign is an absolute essential when it comes to love and relationships. Once
you understand what drives you, nurtures you
and keeps you happy in love, then you can be
true to who you are rather than try to be someone
you're not.

Plus, once you recognise your weak points when
it comes to relationships (and everyone has them),
you can learn to moderate them and focus instead

on boosting your strengths to find happiness in love.

> **KEY CONCEPTS:** late developer, long-lasting commitment, plan your romantic strategy, protect your heart

Cosmic Tip: A relationship is not a business transaction: put your heart and soul into your love life and awaken your passion

When you consider some of the chief Capricorn characteristics, i.e. cool and reserved, patient and respectful, they suggest that you're not the forward type when it comes to dating. In fact, for a typical Capricorn finding love and creating long-lasting relationships can sometimes be a painfully slow process.

You take your time in all areas of life, love included, and you usually want to get to know someone well before you make a move. However, you can be so overly cautious and respectful, fearful even, that you miss out on love or hooking up with the perfect partner because you don't make a move at all.

This is rarely a winning strategy when it comes to dating: hoping and waiting for the other person to come on to you. Therefore, it's right at the start of the game of love that, as a Capricorn, you may have to learn to do things differently.

There is another important factor involved here. Being a Capricorn, sometimes you expect the worst in life. Plus, when it comes to exercising your ego and boasting about your love potential, you're positively averse to it.

This means that someone else can leap in, shouting 'Choose me!', and steal the object of your affection from under your very nose. If you've ever decided not to fight for the one you want and muttered under your breath, 'They probably don't want me anyway,' that's gloomy Capricorn kicking in. Boost your self-esteem, and you increase your love chances.

Making time for dating is another Capricorn conundrum, and it's probably no surprise that many Capricorns can be found dating online. After all, it's an efficient and time-effective way to quickly eliminate no-hopers and line up potential suitors with decent prospects and looks to match. You can also choose the dating site that suits you, whether you're looking for a business type, a millionaire or you're hooking up for sex.

When you're ready for a long-term relationship and you want to settle down, you see this as something of great importance in your life, and you won't enter lightly into any agreement. In fact, this is where your organisational capabilities can kick in, as you're not interested in time-wasters and you've probably already worked out at what age you want to marry and have children.

For the classic Capricorn, working out what's the best way to fit in a relationship can be a puzzle in itself, not to mention possible maternity/paternity leave and how you will continue to make progress up your chosen career ladder. If you're sometimes accused of leaving romance out of the picture, this can be the reason why.

Ultimately, a Capricorn wants to fall in love once in their lifetime and for the relationship to last happily ever after. Which means it's a good idea to draw up a list of essential characteristics for your partner-to-be and ensure you know each other well before sealing the deal.

Commitment means a lot to the average Capricorn and, once you make a wedding vow, you will do your utmost to ensure that your commitment is never broken. You are a loyal and genuine partner, and even if a romantic relationship is also a business transaction in your eyes, it's together for ever.

A partner's prospects matter to you, and you'll be looking for someone who complements you and who shares your long-term goals and dreams. Your partner's reputation is important, because once you're seen as a couple, you want the two of you to look good together.

If your other half can help improve your status and reputation in any way, that's a bonus. Also, you expect your partner to behave respectfully when you're among your peers, whether at work or at play. Secretly, you want your close friends to be impressed by your choice of partner and even be envious.

Once you're in a relationship that's right for you, you'll work hard to provide for and care for your partner's needs. If they want to end it, it's unlikely that you'll accept their decision easily but instead, you'll pull out all the stops to try to keep the two of you together.

If you do end up broken-hearted, it can take you a long time to move on and find another partner. You have a vulnerable side, and once you've been hurt or rejected, you want to protect your feelings. You might prefer to wear a shield of armour around your heart for fear of being hurt again.

Often, the typical Capricorn finds love later in life and tradition states that you're wise to postpone marriage until your first Saturn Return, when you're about twenty-nine or thirty. Sometimes, the Capricorn woman seeks a father figure in love, and the Capricorn man is happy with an older woman by his side.

As you age, however, the youthful, spirited side of your character emerges more and more, which means that as you get older, you might be better suited to a younger, more vibrant partner. When love works well in Capricorn's world, your heart opens, and the right relationship brings you light and joy, healing the dark side of your Saturn nature, which fades with time.

Your Love Matches

Some star signs are a better love match for you than others. The classic combinations are the other two star signs from the same element as your sign, earth; in Capricorn's case, Taurus and Virgo.

If you're a classic alpha Capricorn, it's not always the best idea to look for an alpha partner. Sometimes, opposites not only attract but complement each other too. Look for a partner who's comfortable with their feelings and has a high level of emotional intelligence.

It's also important to recognise that any star sign match can be a good match if you're willing to learn from each other and use astrological insight to understand more about what makes the other person tick. Here's a quick guide to your love matches with all twelve star signs:

Capricorn–Aries: Squaring Up To Each Other

This can be a wicked combination, with each sign bringing out the best (or worst) in one another. It's masculine and competitive, and both signs like to be on top. As long as you know who wears the trousers and that works for both of you, you can be a successful alpha couple.

Capricorn–Taurus: In Your Element

You two can be great mates as well as lovers. You like the good things in life and share a love of designer clothes and status symbols. Fundamentally you know that money isn't everything, and a sense of security creates the sound basis from which this relationship can flourish and grow.

Capricorn–Gemini: Soulmates

Your two star signs may not seem to have much in common, but your dry and offbeat humour resonates with Gemini's wit and love of life. Your wisdom and experience matched with Gemini's thirst for knowledge and insatiable curiosity can work well together.

Capricorn–Cancer: Opposites Attract

You are the worker of the zodiac, who aspires to great things in life and is always looking for a mountain to climb. Cancer needs comfort and nourishment and takes pride in nurturing family and friends. This can be a warm and safe connection if you provide for and protect each other.

Capricorn–Leo: Soulmates

Your sign of Capricorn and majestic Leo are made for each other. The two of you together are a power couple who want to play big, achieve status and make something of your lives. This is a proud combination; two big egos that both need a stage in life upon which to perform.

Capricorn–Virgo: In Your Element

You two share a hard-work ethic and a strong sense of ambition. Working towards common goals helps create a close bond between you. Embrace a goal-oriented lifestyle to ensure you stay in harmony and focus on a mutual awareness of the mind–body–spirit connection.

Capricorn–Libra: Squaring Up To Each Other

This is a fresh and stylish combination, and both of you share a love of good taste, decorum and social niceties. Love and control are in equal measure. A match to admire and be in awe of, but it's what lies underneath the gloss that determines whether your loving bond is real.

Capricorn–Scorpio: Sexy Sextiles

Both of you want to play big in life and feel fulfilled when you're ticking off life goals or significant achievements. Love tends to be a slow burn as neither of you favours a quick fling over a deep and meaningful connection. This combination can grow and mature like a fine wine.

Capricorn–Sagittarius: Next-Door Neighbours

An unlikely combination at first glance; it's not easy to imagine sensible Capricorn and larger-than-life Sagittarius as ideal bedmates. However, both of you are worldly and experienced. If you find a shared ambition or goal, you can work well together and show off your entrepreneurial flair.

Capricorn–Capricorn: Two Peas In A Pod

An elegant and refined match, you two are supremely ambitious and thrive on achievement. You both want to be in control, but you must offer mutual support if the relationship is to flourish. Schedule fun into your busy lives, so love doesn't become all work and no play.

Capricorn–Aquarius: Next-Door Neighbours

You two are at your best out in the world making a difference. You might be too conventional for non-conformist Aquarius, and Aquarius hoards friends like you accumulate trophies. The stereotypical 'odd' match that proves that in love, anything goes.

Capricorn–Pisces: Sexy Sextiles

You have workaholic tendencies, but you also have a quiet and caring demeanour that romantic Pisces feels instinctively. If anyone is going to root out your soft spot, it's mysterious, intuitive Pisces. They act as your muse, and you provide the steady security that Pisces lacks.

Your Sex Life

• • • • •

Let's start by dispelling the myth that Capricorn cares little for sex. Other people might think you're only interested in career and status, and you're too busy for carnal relations, but that's rarely true.

In fact, there are numerous reasons why Capricorn has the potential to be a hot lover. You're an earth sign after all, and earth signs aren't only interested in work and money, they enjoy sensual experiences, physical pleasure included.

Consider your zodiac symbol too, the randy goat, renowned as a symbol of fertility and virility; it's not a horned creature for nothing. Add to this the fact that one of the most debauched festivals of

Roman times, Saturnalia, was named in honour of your planet and their god Saturn. A hat-trick of reasons why sex plays an important role in the Capricorn psyche.

What is important to note, however, is that sex and love don't always go hand in hand as far as you're concerned. You can be quite happy experimenting with sexual activities and not be remotely interested in finding love.

Also, you often have set criteria for your partner in marriage, if that's part of your game plan. Those standards might differ substantially from what you're looking for when it comes to a partner for sex. The controlling type of Capricorn, for example, might be looking for domination games with a sexual partner, whether you're the one holding the whip or vice versa.

Obviously, there's your reputation to think of and some sexual activities might go on behind closed doors or involve a financial transaction. That's not unheard of in Capricorn's experience of life, as you're someone for whom business and pleasure are often completely separate.

For starters, if you have an affair with someone at work, and office sex is not out of the question, the last thing you want is to be fired because of a sexual dalliance. A typical Capricorn's reputation must be upheld at all times.

You do, however, have the potential to be a fantastic lover as you have a reserved exterior but there's a gentle and vulnerable side to your nature. Also, when you find someone you want to be with for more than a one-night stand, you are loyal and tender.

You rarely put yourself first in the bedroom department but, instead, want to ensure that your lover enjoys him/herself completely. After all, you are interested in performance in all areas, and you will be prepared to work hard to ensure the sexual experience isn't over in a flash.

You can be a whizz at self-control, and even if you stick to tried and tested sexual positions, you want to make a lasting impression. Spontaneous sex does have its place in the Capricorn diary, especially if you don't want to sacrifice too much work time for frivolous pleasures.

For ultimate satisfaction, however, it's important that you make time for sex in your schedule so you can give yourself over to the experience 100%. Indulgent, long-lasting lovemaking suits the archetypal Capricorn.

Find yourself a lover who makes you feel totally at ease and enjoy taking part in a slow, sensual exploration of one another's bodies. Only once you're certain of your lover's feelings for you are you willing to open up and explore untapped physical and emotional depths. Sex at its best can become a mystical experience, when you're not only in touch with your inner desires but able to ask for what you want.

48

CAPRICORN ON A FIRST DATE

- you meet after work, looking smart and sophisticated

- you choose the location

- you give marks out of ten for the food, wine, your date

- you talk work and financial prospects

- you have strict criteria if you're to meet again

Your Friends and Family

During childhood, the typical Capricorn is not a natural at making friends. In fact, this can be a lonely time for some Capricorns, and you might prefer to sit with your head in a book rather than hang out with the rest of the gang sharing gossip and anecdotes.

Being one of life's serious folk doesn't lend itself well to being the centre of attention. Also, if you have a harsh inner critic, that's even more reason to back off from social occasions or be the one propping up the wall at school discos. Your self-protective nature kicks in, and sometimes it feels safer to be on your own.

This is perhaps why so many Capricorns resort to humour, because when you're funny, other people want to be your friend. It can be your way into social situations and help to make you feel more at ease and part of a friendship group or social gathering.

When you're not hanging out with friends all the time, you can also indulge your love for learning and your desire to gain knowledge. Many Capricorn children are boffins at heart, and this bodes well for future advancement.

As an adult, you often make good friends through clubs or societies of which you're a member. Finding a person who shares similar interests with you, however niche or outlandish, can be thrilling. When you hook up with a friend who thinks the way you do, this can be the start of a lifelong connection.

A typical Capricorn also veers towards friendship groups that are closely connected to your place of work or a particular hobby or interest. For you, there's a sense of solidarity being around people who you know have similar values to yourself.

If you're an ambitious Capricorn, business networks and political alliances can be the best way to make friendships that are not only sociable and fun but aspirational too. If you have friends or connections who help smooth your path of progress and get you an upgrade in life, this works for you. Plus, you'll have no hesitation in helping other people in return. You gain a lot of fulfilment in life from seeing your friends do well.

Trust is essential in any Capricorn friendship and loyalty is of paramount importance. If someone betrayed you or humiliated you in public, that would quickly kill off any friendship between you.

You can sometimes let friendships drift if you get caught up in your own life. This is a shame, especially if stronger friendships fade away because of a lack of attention. The key to keeping friendships alive is nurturing the emotional connection between you.

You can often be matter-of-fact about relation-ships in general, and sometimes you do what's best for you rather than worry about another person's feelings. If you cancel a get-together at the last minute, for example, you're more likely to convince yourself logically of the reasons why, rather than hold on to any painful emotions.

Old friendships do matter to you, so nurture them well. At the same time, however, acknowledge when you want and need solitude in your life. Being an introvert, you have to find a reason or a purpose for social occasions. Otherwise, you can be more than happy staying at home.

Family usually play a significant role in your life, whether this is your immediate family, your long-lost relations or the people you grew up with. Being a Capricorn, you have deep respect for your elders and the newborn members of the family.

You not only appreciate family ties, but you take on the mantle of responsibility within the household. If your parents were there for you as a child, you're there for them in return when the time comes, to pass on the baton of parenting.

Your resilient and protective nature fits well into family life, and you are a natural provider for the ones you love. You will take on the role of working parent or single parent as and when necessary because you want the best for your family, and your long-term goals will benefit your children as well.

As a parent, you keep strict boundaries, because discipline and rules are part and parcel of the Capricorn parenting package. You have big ambitions for your children and want to bring out the best in them.

You expect them to do well and you can flounder if a child goes off the rails. In family, as in most areas of Capricorn's life, you have high standards and expectations for yourself and your loved ones to live up to.

Your Health and Well-Being

> **KEY CONCEPTS:** regular check-ups, exercise that fits your lifestyle, healthy bones, traditional food, bump up your happiness quota

As a Capricorn, once you realise that a healthy body equals a healthy mind you are more likely to factor regular exercise into your routine. Admittedly, if you're the type of Capricorn who works long hours, finding time to keep fit can be a challenge.

With your excellent discipline levels, however, more likely than not you'll do whatever it takes so you're functioning at your best on all levels. Self-mastery is a Capricorn concept and ideally you want to be strong physically and calm and focused mentally.

The gym is Capricorn's usual exercise venue, preferably one close to work, and weight training is an excellent discipline for you. Running fits well into your schedule too, pounding the pavements before or after work or during your lunchtime.

One area of your body that you need to pay particular attention to is your knees. Anything that impacts too intensively on your knee joints can become a problem over time, so factor in some low impact exercise as well.

Flexibility is important because Capricorn rules the bones. Early-morning stretching helps keep you supple, and yoga benefits your mind, body and soul. The other beneficial exercise for you is swimming, giving the nod to the fishtail of your zodiac symbol.

In fact, swimming can be a meditative experience for you. The rhythmic regularity of the strokes through the water can be relaxing and restorative, as well as boosting your fitness. Too much swimming can be drying for your skin, however, so moisturise regularly and don't make it a daily habit if your skin is sensitive.

Sunbathing can damage your skin in the long run, so wear a good sunscreen at all times. You're not usually a classic sun-worshipper anyway.

For an all-round healthy appearance, look after your teeth and include regular flossing and check-ups at the dentist. If you're a typical Capricorn, you often lean more towards orthodox medicine than alternative treatments. Regular medicals are a good idea for you but don't completely discount options such as acupuncture, supplements and other forms of healing.

There can be times in your life when you're so focused on other areas that you lose sight of yourself and your own needs. In fact, there is a side of the Capricorn nature that can sacrifice self and personal happiness to fulfil a greater goal in life.

If you realise that you've started to neglect your well-being, give your body some special attention. A spa break is the perfect way to replenish your energy levels and pamper yourself too.

As a Capricorn, it's important to keep a close eye on your feelings and notice when your spirits drop. If you start to feel resigned about your life situation, your energy levels are depleted or there's little joy in your life, that's the time to leap into action.

Happiness doesn't always come naturally to you, and there is a side of the Capricorn character that can slip into 'poor me'. If you're starting to sound like Eeyore on a bad day, that's a worry.

Therefore, keep close tabs on your emotional response to life, be around people who brighten up your spirits and actively engage in joyful activities. You could try laughter yoga or book tickets for a comedy show for you and your friends.

Similarly, if you're spending too much time alone and you're starting to feel lonely, do something about it. Use the resilience inherent within your sign to forge strong bonds in life and maintain a disciplined lifestyle that keeps you both healthy and happy.

Capricorn and Food

It's rare to find a Capricorn who's overweight, but that's not to say you are someone who always eats healthily. In fact, sometimes you keep in shape because of the hours you're working or the amount of time you spend running around, burning off calories.

You can get into bad habits due to your lifestyle, whether that's an excess of alcohol, too much caffeine or skipping meals because you're too busy to eat. If you do need to cut back on anything, however, this is where your discipline and will-power kicks in. It's not unusual to find a Capricorn who's teetotal or anti-caffeine. If any addictive substance affects your performance at work, in your eyes that's enough reason to give it up completely.

The Capricorn diet is usually traditional, and you can be quite happy eating a meal that includes meat, potato and two veg. You often prefer a restaurant that serves traditional food and decent portions, rather than somewhere too modern or a dining experience that favours nouvelle cuisine.

Christmas Day falls during Capricorn season, and a classic Christmas dinner is often one of your favourite meals. There's nothing wrong with three courses either in Capricorn's book, unless you want or need to cut back.

Calcium-rich foods, such as dairy, cheese and spinach, are perfect for you because they're good for your bones. If you're a typical Capricorn, you enjoy indulging in rich foods, and ice cream is often favoured by your sign, because it's cold as well as indulgent.

What you eat is often reflected in your skin and this is where a diet that's low in sugar can help you, especially if too many business lunches start to take their toll.

Sometimes you get stuck in a rut when it comes to food, and it's a good idea to plan a schedule for what you're going to eat and when. This is where your Capricorn ability for organisation can revolutionise your eating habits. Either that or get rich enough so you can employ a personal chef to take care of your culinary needs.

Do You Look Like A Capricorn?

Capricorn rules the bones in the body, and your frame tends to be either strong or wiry. You might be the heavy-boned, solid type of Capricorn or the super-toned and lean type. You often have distinctive knees and being knock-kneed is a Capricorn trait.

You come across as having natural authority, and your calm demeanour suggests you mean business. Sometimes you walk with your head down, and your gaze is serious and brooding. When you're in deep thinking mode, it looks as if the weight of the world is on your shoulders.

Your facial definition tends to be distinctive, with a strong jaw and cheekbones to die for. You usually prefer to wear your hair in a classic style, functional rather than fancy. As a Capricorn child, you look older than you are, but you do have an incredible ability to stay looking young as you age.

Your Style and Image

Power-dressing is the ultimate Capricorn uniform, especially when you're ambitious and going places. You suit work clothes, and if your whole wardrobe is geared around a professional look, you won't go far wrong. Even when the dress code is casual, you turn up casual yet smart.

You suit straight lines and traditional, classic styles. You might be wearing jeans and a white shirt, but you will look impeccable, and you have a natural flair for choosing clothes that suit the occasion.

Black is Capricorn's colour, and it suits Capricorn men and women alike. Dark brown, charcoal grey and navy are acceptable colour alternatives for the classic Capricorn. You tend to prefer subtle colours rather than splashing out on bright or multi-coloured outfits.

A typical Capricorn recognises quality, and it is worth investing in a statement suit or investment piece for your wardrobe; an outfit that changes your personality in a good way and makes you feel a million dollars.

Two top Capricorn fashion designers reveal more about Capricorn style. The first is Diane von Furstenberg (31 December), who back in the 1970s designed the iconic wrap dress, an ideal dress of choice for the Capricorn woman.

The second is Carolina Herrera (8 January), who

has dressed more First Ladies than perhaps any other designer. Her look is usually described as 'timeless elegance', and these two words correctly describe the Capricorn style.

Capricorn men are infinitely stylish and often exude old-school glamour. Think of Cary Grant (18 January), Denzel Washington (28 December) and Bradley Cooper (5 January), and you get a sense of the male Capricorn style. All three look great in suits.

Shirts are preferable to T-shirts for both sexes, and the classic Capricorn takes good care of their clothes and accessories. Don't descend into the shabby look, as it doesn't suit you. Being seen in the supermarket wearing tracksuit bottoms and no make-up can be a Capricorn horror story.

Tailored clothes suit you best, and you can carry off heavy fabrics such as tweed and natural fibres like wool and linen. A hot vibrant splash of colour in the shape of a scarf quickly transforms your more sombre, traditional style.

Capricorn rules the skin, so it's wise to spend money on a good moisturiser, and that applies to both sexes. Make-up tends to be dark, and many Capricorn women suit kohl eyeliner. The classic example is Claudia Winkleman (15 January).

Your Home

Your Ideal Capricorn Home:

In a perfect world, you have two homes. A city apartment, highly functional, preferably elevated with a stunning view; and a country house, a quiet retreat away from work. You will naturally employ the top interior designers and stylists to furnish both.

If you're a typical Capricorn, you view your home

and possessions as a sign of status, representing how far you've come and your position in life. You like to impress others, although you do this in a way that's subtle rather than showy. You're rarely interested in the latest fashions and would rather have a home filled with practical yet tasteful features.

Your sign of Capricorn is a traditionalist, and the colours in your home are usually neutral, conservative colours such as navy blue, moss green and your favourite colour, grey.

You might prefer to use heritage paints and choose furniture or ornaments that give the nod to the past, as you tend to love period pieces with a sense of history. Regency-striped wallpaper, a Queen Anne armchair or Shaker furniture would fit perfectly in the classic Capricorn home.

You appreciate quality items, and if you have the budget to match, you'll head straight for exclusive shops with an established reputation to furnish your home. Excellent craft is what you expect from the goods you purchase, and you want quality products that will last. You'll happily pay to keep more expensive items spotlessly clean and serviced regularly.

Dark wood is preferable to light colours, and you love the smell of leather and to see a deep shine to brass and metal trimmings. There won't necessarily be any frills in your home either, as you prefer a classic style.

Plenty of storage is essential, and it must fit in with the general decor. You want everything to be put away neatly, and the smart storage options you go for often say as much about your character as the rest of your home.

If you're a typical Capricorn, you don't want to come back to a messy home, but you recognise that time equals money, so, if you can put your ambitious nature to better use elsewhere, you'll employ a cleaner to keep your home looking spick and span rather than doing it yourself.

Ideally, you will have a room that acts as an office, with a sturdy desk and plenty of room for your books. If not, find a corner of your home that can double up as an office, somewhere to put your briefcase and keep your designer pens; but if possible it's a good idea to have a separate room where you can work quietly.

At the end of a hard day's work, you love to come home and unwind. Classical music appeals to the Capricorn ear, or you might prefer soul, jazz or modern artists. Ideally, you will have the best sound system you can afford and a wide selection of music to listen to.

Your home may be traditional on the whole, but you enjoy having something beautiful to look at. This might be a modern sculpture or classic art that brings a splash of colour to your home.

You can be something of a wine buff too, and you like to share a glass of vintage wine with family or friends at the end of the day. Work often takes precedence over fun in the Capricorn lifestyle, but you still need your downtime and superior, yet comfortable surroundings in which to relax.

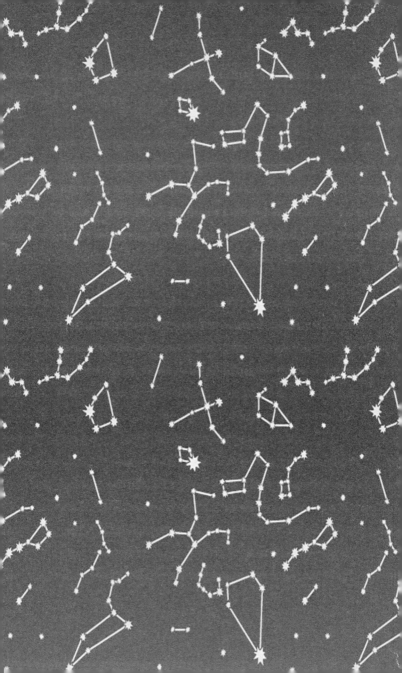

Your Star Sign Destinations

IDEAS FOR CAPRICORN:

- *visit an ashram in India*

- *go mountain-trekking in Nepal*

- *a week at an Oxford university soaking up the culture*

Did you know that many cities and countries are ruled by a particular star sign? This is based on

when a country was founded, although sometimes, depending on their history, places have
more than one star sign attributed to them.

This can help you decide where to go on holiday
and it can also explain why there are certain
places where you feel at home straight away.

Last-minute trips are not your thing as you are
an expert scheduler. In fact, if someone springs
a surprise holiday on you, it can be your worst
nightmare. If it's not already in the diary, it throws
your plans into disarray.

Being a Capricorn you often have a busy schedule,
and you may already have a programme laid out
for the next few weeks, if not until the end of the
year. You much prefer to plan ahead. This means
you tend to get the best deals and you can do
thorough research on the country or city you're
visiting. Preparation is the key to a happy Capricorn
on holiday.

Heading to the mountains is an obvious choice for Capricorn's holiday, in keeping with your zodiac symbol, the mountain goat. If you're typical of your sign, you love walking and anywhere that's high up with a view is ideal. This gives you a broad perspective on the world, and the perfect setting to plan your next ambitious move.

With your workaholic tendencies, it is important to take a complete break from work when you're on holiday. Somewhere in the middle of nature is perfect, preferably quiet with few people around.

It might freak you out to have a complete digital detox, but it's the best thing for you. There are times in your life when you need silence and solitude, so don't be afraid of spending time alone.

Family members are often factored into your holiday plans, and you might decide to take an elderly parent or a child or younger relative to a destination they'll love. This gives you an opportunity to spend quality time together as well as impart your wisdom. You have an uncanny ability to steer and influence your loved ones in the right direction.

Countries ruled by Capricorn include India, Mexico, West Indies, Lithuania, Albania, Bulgaria

Cities ruled by Capricorn include Oxford in the UK; Delhi in India; Mexico City; Brussels in Belgium

Your Career and Vocation

KEY CONCEPTS: the empire builder, responsibility and status, tradition and convention, take a sabbatical

Your sign of Capricorn has many qualities that translate admirably to the world of business, power and status. If you're going to take on a top position in an established and respected profession, it helps to be an individual who understands inherently the vital roles of responsibility and dignity.

Capricorn is a cardinal sign that denotes leadership, and your element of earth is grounded and stable. Other people often feel in safe hands when your sign is in charge.

You have a deep respect for duty and commitment, and you take any role of responsibility seriously, whether you're the chair of the preschool committee or you run the International Monetary Fund. That position, incidentally, is currently held by a Capricorn, Christine Lagarde (1 January).

Sometimes, as a Capricorn, you end up in a job for years and years and win the award for the longest-serving employee. Loyalty comes naturally to you, and the classic Capricorn respects authority. If you believe in the business you're working for, and you're treated fairly and respectfully, you see no reason to move on.

It is important, however, that you have a sense of purpose within your chosen career or vocation. Without a long-term goal or endgame to keep you motivated, you can quickly lose interest.

Similarly, you fare best in a role or job where there's clear evidence of the progress you're making and you can move up the career or status ladder. Having a new goal to aim for is imperative for Capricorn.

At your best, you are hard-working and one of life's grafters and you have the capability to be disciplined and controlled. For some Capricorns, work is everything, and it can become an obsession, your reason for living.

You throw your heart and soul into your chosen profession and will work all the hours necessary and do whatever it takes to be successful. This can sometimes be to the detriment of other areas of your life, such as close relationships and socialising. It's important not to make the mistake of sacrificing your personal life for your career, as it can be lonely at the top.

You can be a hard taskmaster too, if you rise to a position of influence and you expect your employees to be as disciplined and committed as you are. If you're to govern well, you need to be more tolerant of others and keep your expectations realistic. Inject warmth and fun into the work environment so it doesn't lose its appeal for other people, or yourself.

You are good at taking control, however, and you usually have excellent organisational skills. You're rarely scared of big business or stepping into a new role of responsibility, and this can be a real bonus for you.

The ultimate Capricorn position is having your own empire that you can run the way you choose. It might be a small business with significant potential or a profession or mission that you make your own.

There are countless examples of Capricorns renowned for their excellence and superiority in their chosen field, such as Greek shipping magnate Aristotle Onassis (20 January), whose name is synonymous with wealth and prestige; mafia boss Al Capone (17 January) and Martin Luther King (15 January), activist and leader in the Civil Rights movement.

Martin Luther King famously said 'I have a dream' and when you recognise your purpose and mission in life, anything is possible. Find your niche, find what you're good at and utilise your Capricorn abilities to be the best you can be.

Usually, you go for careers or roles in life that are traditional and conventional, and you like to play by the rules and do things properly. You appreciate the hierarchy in a company or an established way of doing things.

Sometimes, you have to be careful not to stay stuck in a job or hold on too tightly to tradition.

Progress is part of the modern way of life, so keep up to date with new technologies and ideas and be willing to embrace fresh thinking and innovative solutions, whatever your career or role.

It's also helpful for you to keep a healthy work/life balance and this doesn't always come naturally. If you spend some years of your life working hard towards a specific or major life goal, ensure you then stop and give yourself a break before you move on to the next thing.

It's in the quiet moments, the solitude, that you can tap into a deeper side of your Capricorn character. Think about taking a sabbatical or remove yourself from the cut and thrust of the work environment and dip into nature. You might find that your best ideas come when you stop working altogether.

If you're seeking inspiration for a new job, take a look at the list below, which reveals the traditional careers that come under the Capricorn archetype:

TRADITIONAL CAPRICORN CAREERS

doctor

osteopath

dentist

CEO/director

chief constable

senior civil servant

business owner

professional organiser

head teacher

careers officer

security guard

music roadie

probate solicitor

appraiser

historian

archaeologist

classics lecturer

obituary writer

vineyard owner

spiritual guru

Your Money and Prosperity

You have all the correct star sign criteria for doing well with money. Firstly, you are one of the three earth signs, which focus on the real world, including financial and material security.

Being financially secure is important to you, and you need a safe base if you're to perform well. Once you're not worrying about where the next paycheque is going to come from, then you can allow your ambitious nature full rein.

Firstly, earth signs are practical and good with facts and figures. It's rare that you would bury your head in the sand around money and leave bills unopened. Instead, you're more likely to know what you've got in your bank account and your budget for the coming month.

Secondly, you're one of the cardinal signs, the leaders of the zodiac, so you're goal-oriented and in your case, this is closely linked to your ambition and status in life. If you're a typical Capricorn, you want to do well financially so you can afford the lifestyle that suits you.

Add to this a disciplined nature and a love of planning, and you're set up to be a saver rather than a spender. You often defer instant gratification for long-term fulfilment and satisfaction.

You're not usually flashy, but you do appreciate quality goods and status. If you're in a responsible position, you want to dress accordingly and ensure that you have the appropriate symbols of success. This might include an expensive watch, the latest mobile phone, a designer car. It matters to you that you fit in and look the part.

This can develop into 'keeping up with the Joneses', but even on a smaller scale, it means having the designer brand that's 'in' or a similar outfit to friends and acquaintances. Rebel and outrageous are two words that rarely describe the Capricorn nature.

If you're dealt the right hand in life, combined with a calculated plan for how to play your cards strategically, you can end up being wealthy or at least well off. If you speculate with money, you do so wisely, and you won't take a risk without researching everything thoroughly.

Keep to what you know, e.g. if you're a savvy corporate Capricorn, invest in start-up companies or business stocks and shares. If you're doing well, you won't stop either but will line up new money-making initiatives one after the other, and you do learn from your mistakes.

Having a responsible attitude to money means that you don't always have a reputation for being the most generous of friends. If anyone's going to quibble over who paid for what on a night out, it's a Capricorn.

If you find yourself turning into Scrooge and becoming miserly, or you allow fear to hold you back from treating yourself or others, then it might be time to stop and question your philosophy on life.

As a Capricorn, you excel at saving for the future or building a portfolio that will bring a significant return in the long run, but don't miss out on enjoying the present day. Sometimes you have one foot in the past and one foot in the future when you would do better from having both feet firmly planted in the here and now.

Your Cosmic Gifts and Talents

Be The Greatest

When you find your passion in life, the talent you're good at that you love more than anything else, you have every opportunity of turning your Capricorn capabilities to the optimum performance. You are in turn determined, hard-working, resilient, ambitious and disciplined. Add this together – talent and drive – and you can go far. Two Capricorn icons who deserve the title 'the greatest' are Elvis Presley (8 January) and Muhammad Ali (17 January). You're a Capricorn – be the best you can be, be the greatest!

Draw Up A Plan

You have the patience and diligence to plan and stay on track with your long-term goals. The classic Capricorn is rarely a one-hit wonder or a get-rich-quick merchant, but instead, you deliver your long game. This is where you excel in life, so draw up a five- or ten-year plan, start a savings scheme or give your backing to a long-term political, social or community initiative. Find the acorn of today that you can grow into the oak tree of tomorrow.

Show Respect

If you're a typical Capricorn, you know how to play by the rules, and you are respectful of authority. Essentially, you are the face of dignity in a world where unruliness and chaos fight for dominance. Your ability to stand firm in the face of crisis and to be resilient no matter what's thrown at you can be a valuable lesson for others. Your planet Saturn is linked not only to time but also to karma, and the phrase 'You reap what you sow' could have been written for a Capricorn. Show respect and keep your moral beliefs and integrity intact.

Walk The Path Of Spirit

The symbol of the mountain is synonymous with ambition and achieving work goals in the Capricorn lexicon. There is, however, another reason to go up the mountain: so you can get to the top and sit down, through the night if necessary. This is one way to practise solitude and silence, to listen to the wisdom of the universe and walk the path of spirit.

This is the path of Capricorn shaman Carlos Castaneda (25 December), who documented his own shamanic experiences in *The Teachings of*

Don Juan, TM (transcendental meditation) advocate David Lynch (20 January) and the poetic voice of singer-songwriter Patti Smith (30 December).

Honour Tradition

History and tradition, legacy and heritage are tightly woven into your Capricorn DNA. You were born to be a symbol of permanence in an impermanent world and to honour tradition. You can do this by writing your memoirs, discovering your family tree or finding out more about your heritage. Similarly, celebrate religious festivals and acknowledge important family dates. Leave a legacy from your life or write your obituary. You were born as the old year ends and a new year begins, an ideal time to reflect on the past and build new dreams for the future.

Funny Bones

As a Capricorn, you often have a great sense of humour, which seems strange considering that your ruling planet is Saturn, the Darth Vader of the universe. Perhaps it's the phrase 'If you don't laugh, you'll cry' that resonates for the typical Capricorn, or maybe it's your higher-than-average intelligence that means you rise above the absurdities of life through humour.

There are many Sun Capricorns who have been successful in the world of comedy: Tracey Ullman (30 December), Caroline Aherne (24 December), Rowan Atkinson (6 January) and Rob Delaney (19 January) to name a few. Share your wry sense of humour and droll wit with the world, whether you're making other people laugh or yourself. Flex those funny bones.

Saturn Returns

The planet Saturn is intrinsically linked to critical stages in life. It takes Saturn twenty-nine or thirty years to make one circuit of the zodiac and in astrology this is called your Saturn Return. The first Return, when you're thirty, is the astrological coming-of-age, a step up into adulthood. Capricorns rarely flourish before this key event. The second Return, when you're sixty, is a time of retirement perhaps, when you're coming to terms with the ageing process. Many Capricorns start a new career or learn a new skill at this age.

The third Return, when you're ninety, can still be a time of achievement for relentless Capricorn. Betty White (17 January 1922) has the longest TV career of any female entertainer, fitting for her Capricorn status. She won her first Emmy nomination in 1951, close to her first Saturn Return, and in 2011, when she was nearing her third Saturn Return, she was once again nominated for an Emmy. A true Capricorn!

Films, Books, Music

• • • • •

Films: *Casablanca* starring Humphrey Bogart (25 December) or the Lord Of The Rings trilogy, from the books by J. R. R. Tolkien (3 January)

Books: *The Catcher In The Rye* by J. D. Salinger (1 January), the Twilight book series by Stephenie Meyer (24 December) or any of the books starring Winnie-the-Pooh by A. A. Milne (18 January)

Music: 'Big Spender' by Shirley Bassey (8 January) or 'Heroes' by David Bowie (8 January) or 'Suspicious Minds' by Elvis Presley (8 January). Are you a Capricorn born on 8 January? Start singing lessons now!

YOGA POSE:

Mountain: improves posture, strengthens the
joints and steadies breathing

TAROT CARD:

The Hermit

GIFTS TO BUY A CAPRICORN:

- designer briefcase
- luxury food hamper
- a tailored shirt
- art or wine as an investment
- teeth-whitening treatment
- watch or grandfather clock
- monogrammed scarf
- hiking boots
- membership to an elite club
- Star Gift – a trust fund

Capricorn Celebrities Born On Your Birthday

DECEMBER

22 Ralph Fiennes, Noel Edmonds, Vanessa Paradis, Meghan Trainor

23 Carol Ann Duffy, Trisha Goddard, Corey Haim, Tara Palmer-Tomkinson, Carla Bruni-Sarkozy, Eddie Vedder, Holly Madison

CAPRICORN

24 Howard Hughes, Ava Gardner, Carol
Vorderman, Wade Williams, Barry
Chuckle, Caroline Aherne, Ricky Martin,
Ryan Seacrest, Louis Tomlinson,
Stephenie Meyer

25 Carlos Castaneda, Humphrey Bogart,
Conrad Hilton, Justin Trudeau, Sissy
Spacek, Annie Lennox, Helena
Christensen, Dido, Nadiya Hussain, Kenny
Everett

26 Henry Miller, Steve Allen, Lars Ulrich,
Jared Leto, Kit Harington

27 Marlene Dietrich, Janet Street-Porter,
Gerard Depardieu, Masi Oka, Salman
Khan, Lily Cole

28 Maggie Smith, Denzel Washington,
Sienna Miller, Joe Manganiello, John
Legend, Nigel Kennedy

29 Jon Voight, Patricia Clarkson, Mary Tyler Moore, Ted Danson, Jude Law

31 Rudyard Kipling, Bo Diddley, Matt Lauer, Davy Jones, Tracey Ullman, Tiger Woods, Patti Smith, LeBron James, Ellie Goulding, Jay Kay

31 Anthony Hopkins, Alex Ferguson, John Denver, Ben Kingsley, Val Kilmer, Ricky Whittle, Donna Summer, Psy, Diane von Furstenberg, Simon Wiesenthal

JANUARY

1 J. D. Salinger, J. Edgar Hoover, Christine Lagarde, Frank Langella, Lauren Silverman

2 Isaac Asimov, David Bailey, Todd Haynes, Gabrielle Carteris, Cuba Gooding Jr, Christy Turlington, Kate Bosworth, Rob Beckett

3 J. R. R. Tolkien, Sergio Leone, Victor Borge, Mel Gibson, Michael Schumacher, John Thaw

4 Isaac Newton, Louis Braille, Michael Stipe

5 Robert Duvall, Lee Van Cleef, Diane Keaton, Vinnie Jones, Marilyn Manson, Bradley Cooper, January Jones, Suki Waterhouse

6 Joan of Arc, Benjamin Franklin, John DeLorean, Alan Watts, Trudie Styler, Rowan Atkinson, Angus Deayton, Anthony Minghella, Nigella Lawson, Irina Shayk, Eddie Redmayne, Syd Barrett, Alex Turner, A. R. Rahman

7 Christian Louboutin, David Caruso, Nicolas Cage, Lewis Hamilton, Katie Couric, Ruth Negga, Jeremy Renner, Irrfan Khan, Blue Ivy Carter

8 Elvis Presley, Shirley Bassey, Stephen Hawking, David Bowie, R. Kelly, Carolina Herrera

9 Richard Nixon, Simone de Beauvoir, Joan Baez, Jimmy Page, Imelda Staunton, Joely Richardson, Catherine Duchess of Cambridge, Nina Dobrev

10 Rod Stewart, George Foreman, Abbey Clancy, Cash Warren, Jared Kushner

11 John Sessions, Mary J. Blige, Jamelia, Amanda Peet

12 Swami Vivekananda, Joe Frazier, Michael Aspel, Haruki Murakami, Howard Stern, Kirstie Alley, Rob Zombie, Olivier Martinez, Keith Anderson, Heather Mills, Mel C., Zayn Malik, Jeff Bezos, Pixie Lott

13 Charles Nelson Reilly, Julia Louis-Dreyfus, Trace Adkins, Patrick Dempsey, Orlando Bloom, Liam Hemsworth, Bill Bailey

14 Cecil Beaton, Steven Soderbergh, Faye Dunaway, Richard Briers, Hugh Fearnley-Whittingstall, LL Cool J, Emily Watson, Karen Elson, Dave Grohl

15 Aristotle Onassis, Martin Luther King, James Nesbitt, Claudia Winkleman, Pete Waterman, Pitbull

16 Laura Schlessinger, Susan Sontag, Kate Moss, Aaliyah, Sade, FKA Twigs

17 Al Capone, Muhammad Ali, Betty White, Eartha Kitt, Andy Kaufman, Steve Harvey, Paul Merton, Jim Carrey, Naveen Andrews, Kid Rock, Zooey Deschanel, Michelle Obama, Françoise Hardy, Calvin Harris

18 Cary Grant, Danny Kaye, Kevin Costner, Jane Horrocks, Mark Rylance

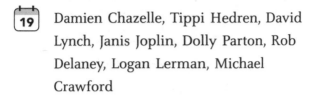

19 Damien Chazelle, Tippi Hedren, David Lynch, Janis Joplin, Dolly Parton, Rob Delaney, Logan Lerman, Michael Crawford

20 David Lynch, Gary Barlow

Q&A Section

• • • • •

Q. What is the difference between a Sun sign and a Star sign?

A. They are the same thing. The Sun spends one month in each of the twelve star signs every year, so if you were born on 1 January, you are a Sun Capricorn. In astronomy, the Sun is termed a star rather than a planet, which is why the two names are interchangeable. The term 'zodiac sign', too, means the same as Sun sign and Star sign and is another way of describing which one of the twelve star signs you are, e.g. Sun Capricorn.

Q. What does it mean if I'm born on the cusp?

A. Being born on the cusp means that you were born on a day when the Sun moves from one of the twelve zodiac signs into the next. However, the Sun doesn't change signs at the same time each year. Sometimes it can be a day earlier or a day later. In the celebrity birthday section of the book, names in brackets mean that this person's birthday falls into this category.

If you know your complete birth data, including the date, time and place you were born, you can find out definitively what Sun sign you are. You do this by either checking an ephemeris (a planetary table) or asking an astrologer. For example, if a baby were born on 20 January 2018, it would be Sun Capricorn if born before 03:09 GMT or Sun Aquarius if born after 03:09 GMT. A year earlier, the Sun left Capricorn a day earlier and entered Aquarius on 19 January 2017, at 21:24 GMT. Each year the time changes are slightly different.

Q. Has my sign of the zodiac changed since I was born?

A. Every now and again, the media talks about a new sign of the zodiac called Ophiuchus and about there now being thirteen signs. This means that you're unlikely to be the same Sun sign as you always thought you were.

This method is based on fixing the Sun's movement to the star constellations in the sky, and is called 'sidereal' astrology. It's used traditionally in India and other Asian countries.

The star constellations are merely namesakes for the twelve zodiac signs. In western astrology, the zodiac is divided into twelve equal parts that are in sync with the seasons. This method is called 'tropical' astrology. The star constellations and the zodiac signs aren't the same.

Astrology is based on a beautiful pattern of symmetry (see Additional Information) and it wouldn't be the same if a thirteenth sign were introduced into the pattern. So never fear, no one is going to have to say their star sign is Ophiuchus, a name nobody even knows how to pronounce!

Q. Is astrology still relevant to me if I was born in the southern hemisphere?

A. Yes, astrology is unquestionably relevant to you. Astrology's origins, however, were founded in the northern hemisphere, which is why the Spring Equinox coincides with the Sun's move into Aries, the first sign of the zodiac. In the southern hemisphere, the seasons are reversed. Babylonian, Egyptian and Greek and Roman astrology are the forebears of modern-day astrology, and all of these civilisations were located in the northern hemisphere.

• • • • •

Q. Should I read my Sun sign, Moon sign and Ascendant sign?

A. If you know your horoscope or you have drawn up an astrology wheel for the time of your birth, you will be aware that you are more than your Sun sign. The Sun is the most important star in the sky, however, because the other planets revolve around it, and your horoscope in the media is based on Sun signs. The Sun represents your essence, who you are striving to become throughout your lifetime.

The Sun, Moon and Ascendant together give you a broader impression of yourself as all three reveal further elements about your personality. If you know your Moon and Ascendant signs, you can read all three books to gain further insight into who you are. It's also a good idea to read the Sun sign book that relates to your partner, parents, children, best friends, even your boss for a better understanding of their characters too.

Q. Is astrology a mix of fate and free will?

A. Yes. Astrology is not causal, i.e. the planets don't cause things to happen in your life; instead, the two are interconnected, hence the saying 'As above, so below'. The symbolism of the planets' movements mirrors what's happening on earth and in your personal experience of life.

You can choose to sit back and let your life unfold, or you can decide the best course of action available to you. In this way, you are combining your fate and free will, and this is one of astrology's major purposes in life. A knowledge of astrology can help you live more authentically, and it offers you a fresh perspective on how best to make progress in your life.

Q. What does it mean if I don't identify with my Sun sign? Is there a reason for this?

A. The majority of people identify with their Sun sign, and it is thought that one route to fulfilment is to grow into your Sun sign. You do get the odd exception, however.

For example, a Pisces man was adamant that he wasn't at all romantic, mystical, creative or caring, all typical Pisces archetypes. It turned out he'd spent the whole of his adult life working in the oil industry and lived primarily on the sea. Neptune is one of Pisces' ruling planets and god of the sea and Pisces rules all liquids, including oil. There's the Pisces connection.

Q. What's the difference between astrology and astronomy?

A. Astrology means 'language of the stars', whereas astronomy means 'mapping of the stars'. Traditionally, they were considered one discipline, one form of study and they coexisted together for many hundreds of years. Since the dawn of the Scientific Age, however, they have split apart.

Astronomy is the scientific strand, calculating and logging the movement of the planets, whereas astrology is the interpretation of the movement of the stars. Astrology works on a symbolic and intuitive level to offer guidance and insight. It reunites you with a universal truth, a knowingness that can sometimes get lost in place of an objective, scientific truth. Both are of value.

Q. What is a cosmic marriage in astrology?

A. One of the classic indicators of a relation-ship that's a match made in heaven is the union of the Sun and Moon. When they fall close to each other in the same sign in the birth charts of you and your partner, this is called a cosmic marriage. In astrology, the Sun and Moon are the king and queen of the heavens; the Sun is a masculine energy, and the Moon a feminine energy. They represent the eternal cycle of day and night, yin and yang.

Q. What does the Saturn Return mean?

A. In traditional astrology, Saturn was the furthest planet from the Sun, representing boundaries and the end of the universe. Saturn is linked to karma and time, and represents authority, structure and responsibility. It takes Saturn twenty-nine to thirty years to make a complete cycle of the zodiac and return to the place where it was when you were born.

This is what people mean when they talk about their Saturn Return; it's the astrological coming of age. Turning thirty can be a soul-searching time, when you examine how far you've come in life and whether you're on the right track. It's a watershed moment, a reality check and a defining stage of adulthood. The decisions you make during your Saturn Return are crucial, whether they represent endings or new commitments. Either way, it's the start of an important stage in your life path.

Additional Information

• • • • •

THE SYMMETRY OF ASTROLOGY

There is a beautiful symmetry to the zodiac (see horoscope wheel). There are twelve zodiac signs, which can be divided into two sets of 'introvert' and 'extrovert' signs, four elements (fire, earth, air, water), three modes (cardinal, fixed, mutable) and six pairs of opposite signs.

One of the values of astrology is in bringing opposites together, showing how they complement each other and work together and, in so doing, restore unity. The horoscope wheel represents the cyclical nature of life.

Aries (*March 21–April 19*)
Taurus (*April 20–May 20*)
Gemini (*May 21–June 20*)
Cancer (*June 21–July 22*)
Leo (*July 23–August 22*)
Virgo (*August 23–September 22*)
Libra (*September 23–October 23*)
Scorpio (*October 24–November 22*)
Sagittarius (*November 23–December 21*)
Capricorn (*December 22–January 20*)
Aquarius (*January 21–February 18*)
Pisces (*February 19–March 20*)

ELEMENTS

There are four elements in astrology and three signs allocated to each. The elements are:

fire – Aries, Leo, Sagittarius
earth – Taurus, Virgo, Capricorn
air – Gemini, Libra, Aquarius
water – Cancer, Scorpio, Pisces

What each element represents:

Fire – fire blazes bright and fire types are inspirational, motivational, adventurous and love creativity and play

Earth – earth is grounding and solid, and earth rules money, security, practicality, the physical body and slow living

Air – air is intangible and vast and air rules thinking, ideas, social interaction, debate and questioning

Water – water is deep and healing and water rules feelings, intuition, quietness, relating, giving and sharing

MODES

There are three modes in astrology and four star signs allocated to each. The modes are:

cardinal – Aries, Cancer, Libra, Capricorn
fixed – Taurus, Leo, Scorpio, Aquarius
mutable – Gemini, Virgo, Sagittarius, Pisces

What each mode represents:

Cardinal – The first group represents the leaders of the zodiac, and these signs love to initiate and take action. Some say they're controlling.

Fixed – The middle group holds fast and stands the middle ground and acts as a stable, reliable companion. Some say they're stubborn.

Mutable – The last group is more willing to go with the flow and let life drift. They're more flexible and adaptable and often dual-natured. Some say they're all over the place.

INTROVERT AND EXTROVERT SIGNS/ OPPOSITE SIGNS

The introvert signs are the earth and water signs and the extrovert signs are the fire and air signs. Both sets oppose each other across the zodiac.

The 'introvert' earth and water oppositions are:

- Taurus – • Scorpio
- Cancer – • Capricorn
- Virgo – • Pisces

The 'extrovert' air and fire oppositions are:

- Aries – • Libra
- Gemini – • Sagittarius
- Leo – • Aquarius

THE HOUSES

The houses of the astrology wheel are an additional component to Sun sign horoscopes. The symmetry that is inherent within astrology remains, as the wheel is divided into twelve equal sections, called 'houses'. Each of the twelve houses is governed by one of the twelve zodiac signs.

There is an overlap in meaning as you move round the houses. Once you know the symbolism of all the star signs, it can be fleshed out further by learning about the areas of life represented by the twelve houses.

The houses provide more specific information if you choose to have a detailed birth chart reading.

This is based not only on your day of birth, which reveals your star sign, but also your time and place of birth. Here's the complete list of the meanings of the twelve houses and the zodiac sign they are ruled by:

1 – **Aries:** self, physical body, personal goals

2 – **Taurus:** money, possessions, values

3 – **Gemini:** communication, education, siblings, local neighbourhood

4 – **Cancer:** home, family, roots, the past, ancestry

5 – **Leo:** creativity, romance, entertainment, children, luck

6 – **Virgo:** work, routine, health, service

7 – **Libra:** relationships, the 'other', enemies, contracts

8 – **Scorpio:** joint finances, other people's resources, all things hidden and taboo

9 – **Sagittarius:** travel, study, philosophy, legal affairs, publishing, religion

10 – **Capricorn:** career, vocation, status, reputation

11 – **Aquarius:** friends, groups, networks, social responsibilities

12 – **Pisces:** retreat, sacrifice, spirituality

A GUIDE TO LOVE MATCHES

The star signs relate to each other in different ways depending on their essential nature. It can also be helpful to know the pattern they create across the zodiac. Here's a quick guide that relates to the chapter on Love Matches:

Two Peas In A Pod – the same star sign

Opposites Attract – star signs opposite each other

Soulmates – five or seven signs apart, and a traditional 'soulmate' connection

In Your Element – four signs apart, which means you share the same element

Squaring Up To Each Other – three signs apart, which means you share the same mode

Sexy Sextiles – two signs apart, which means you're both 'introverts' or 'extroverts'

Next Door Neighbours – one sign apart, different in nature but often share close connections